YOUR KNOWLEDGE HAS VALUE

- We will publish your bachelor's and
  master's thesis, essays and papers

- Your own eBook and book -
  sold worldwide in all relevant shops

- Earn money with each sale

Upload your text at www.GRIN.com
and publish for free

Arthur Landsman

The Lawrence Allen Revitalization Project

.

GRIN Publishing

Imprint:

Copyright © 2013 GRIN Verlag GmbH
Print and binding: Books on Demand GmbH, Norderstedt Germany
ISBN: 978-3-656-86877-4

This book at GRIN:

http://www.grin.com/en/e-book/286590/the-lawrence-allen-revitalization-project

GRIN - Your knowledge has value

Since its foundation in 1998, GRIN has specialized in publishing academic texts by students, college teachers and other academics as e-book and printed book. The website www.grin.com is an ideal platform for presenting term papers, final papers, scientific essays, dissertations and specialist books.

Visit us on the internet:

http://www.grin.com/

http://www.facebook.com/grincom

http://www.twitter.com/grin_com

The Lawrence Allen Revitalization Project

Scholarly Research Paper

PASC 200
Project Management
October 13, 2013

The Lawrence Allen neighbourhood, which was built in the post-war years using high-density building design, is facing new challenges in today's society. Years of neglect and poor design layout have resulted in unsuitable conditions for habitation by its current tenants. The majority of the housing in the neighbourhood is in declining physical condition and requires replacement or renewal to provide current residents with an acceptable standard of living. Toronto's population is also expected to grow in the next two decades which will facilitate the need for new housing in the city. The area represents one of Toronto's inner-city areas, which contain some of the city's most economically disadvantaged residents. The revitalization of the Lawrence-Allen area and the Lawrence Heights community provides the opportunity for social and economic change in this economically marginalized neighbourhood. It will allow for a previously isolated and disconnected neighbourhood to integrate back into the broader community. Through public and private investment the revitalization of the Lawrence-Allen area will increase the quality of life in the urban core, decrease high crime rates, and provide new housing for Toronto's projected population growth.

As reported in the Toronto Star, the article "Massive Plan to Revamp Troubled Lawrence Heights," articulates that the Lawrence Heights neighbourhood, which is currently a low-income housing project, known as "The Jungle," suffers from high rates of criminal activity and destitution, and is set to be revitalized as part of the Lawrence-Allen Revitalization Project into a newly livable, environmentally friendly, pedestrian community with new mixed-income housing, new parks, retail and commercial centres, and schools. The area in question covers approximately 340 hectares between Lawrence Avenue West, Bathurst Street, Dufferin Street, and Highway 401.[1] The core area of the revitalization covers 75 hectares of land, and encompasses the aforementioned "Toronto Community Housing's Lawrence Heights neighbourhood and lands owned by the Toronto District School Board, the City of Toronto, and Riocan."[2] It is similar in scale to the revitalization project currently in progress in the Regent Park area. Both areas share similar tenant populations, demographic profiles, crime and gang statistics, and design of land as well. Approximately 7,500 tenants were residing in the Regent Park development area before the revitalization project began, compared to 3,500 currently living in Lawrence Heights.[3] The plan is expected to be a long-term development of 20 years, which will include a mixed-income, mixed-use community with housing, employment, social and recreational opportunities for all of the communities residents. It will renew and increase the current stock of government housing in the area, build new public infrastructure, improve community facilities and municipal infrastructure as

1

well as active parks, and schools, and redevelop a balanced transportation system which prioritizes pedestrians, cyclists and transit users.

The Lawrence-Allen area falls into a desirable area of land in the urban core of Toronto with a close proximity to the city's downtown. It has been identified by the City of Toronto as one of the city's "Priority Neighbourhoods" in need of social and infrastructure improvements.[4] Instead of remaining a concentration of government housing, a mixed-housing plan will be introduced to the area with public and private owned housing, as well as commercial and transportation development. The subsequent reduction of the subsidized units, and creation of new rental and owner units will bring in more revenue for the city in addition to the other revitalization objectives mentioned. The project is similar in scale to the Regent Park revitalization project, which saw a reduction of the area's proportion of assisted units from 100 per cent to 30 per cent.[5] Once completed, the redeveloped Lawrence Heights community will serve as a model of inner-city community housing design for future revitalization projects in the city of Toronto.

Project Phases

There is expected to be four major phases for the project over a 20-year lifecycle:

Phase 1: 2012 – 2016

Estimated New Market Units: 800 – 1000, Estimated TCHC Replacement Units: 233, Parks and Facilities: New neighbourhood park, Baycrest park improvements, potential facilities in new buildings at Allen/Ranee intersection, potential new and/or replacement Child Care centres.[6]

Phase 2: 2017 – 2021

Estimated New Market Units 800-900, Estimated TCHC Replacement Units: 213, Parks and Facilities: New community park (east side), rebuilt Flemington elementary school, potential new community recreation centre and pool, potential facilities along Flemington road, renovations to Barbara Frum library, potential new or replacement child care centre.[7]

Phase 3: 2022 – 2026

Estimated New Market Units 1300 – 1400, Estimated TCHC Replacement Units: 377, Parks and Facilities: New community park (west side), new TCDSB elementary school, potential New Community Recreation Centre and pool, potential new replacement Child Care centres.[8]

Phase 4: 2027 – 2030

Estimated New Market Units 1400 -1500, Estimated TCHC Replacement Units: 385,

Parks and Facilities: Potential facilities along Flemington Road, potential new replacement child care.[9]

Other Phases: Lawrence Square Mall and Bathurst Heights

Estimated New Market Units: 1200 – 1500, Parks and Facilities: New neighbourhood park, potential replacement of existing community facility space, potential new non-profit facility hub, redeveloped secondary school with schoolyard, other potential facilities located with school include pool and child care if not addressed in other phases.[10]

The total new market units for each phase equates to approximately 5500-6300 plus the total TCHC replacement units 1208, for a grand total after the 20-year development cycle is completed of 6700-7500 units.[11]

The project is currently in the planning stage of the Project Life Cycle. Project objectives have already been defined and established by the project's management staff. The scheduling of the phases of the project is currently taking place, with decisions being made as to when to begin construction. The preliminary budget has also been completed, with a further secondary budget to shortly follow, as well as associated implementation plans and staff reports. Each project phase represents a milestone in the project's lifecycle. These milestones are crucial points in the project development timeline, where review can take place.

Being such a large and complex project, it has been in development since 2005 when Toronto City Council designated "Lawrence Heights as one of 13 priority neighbourhoods targeted for infrastructure investment and community service improvement."[12] In 2008, planning initiatives by the City of Toronto, Toronto Community Housing Corporation (TCHC), and Toronto District School Board (TDSB) began in the form of a two year coordinated planning study. This plan, which was completed in 2010, has formed the basis for the current Secondary Plan which is currently nearing completion.

3

Time and Cost Requirements

The plan is expected to be completed in a 20-year period of development and cost a minimum of $240.60 million. The first phase of the project is expected to commence in 2012, with four phases of development and an excepted completion date around the year 2030. The first phase is expected to cost approximately $40.33 million, the second phase $95.77 million, the third phase $61.90 million and the last phase is projected to cost $40.24 million. Although the final budget of the revitalization project has not been set, a preliminary analysis and budget can be seen in the table below:

Table 1:	Lawrence Allen Revitalization Plan – Preliminary Order of Magnitude Costs (In $000s)					
	Short term	Phase 1 (2012-2016)	Phase 2 (2017 – 2021)	Phase 3 (2022 – 2026)	Phase 4 (2027 - 2030)	Total
Road & Above Grade Infrastructure	$2.350	$ 5.300	$39.500	$14.800	$26.650	$ 88.600
Water, Wastewater & Below Grade Infrastructure		$23.400	$ 5.400	$15.650	$12.400	$ 56.850
Parks and Greenway		$ 7.060	$ 7.630	$ 3.575	$ 1.190	$ 19.455
Community Recreation Facilities		$ .675	$291545	$23.980		$ 54.200
Other Facilities		$ 3.900	$13.700	$ 3.900		$ 21.500
Total	$2.350	$40.335	$95.775	$61.905	$40.240	$240.605
Note:	All costs are in 2010 dollars. No escalation or inflation factors were applied.					[13]

Source: The City of Toronto, City Planning, *Lawrence Allen Revitalization Plan Staff Report – June 3, 2010*, Sept. 2010, Web, table 1.

Also, the following assumptions have been considered during formulation of the table:

"Costs are:

Based on 2010 dollars;

Include a 15% engineering fee;

Include a 30% contingency;

Include the removal of existing municipal infrastructure;

Exclude the removal, replacement, relocation and installation of utility infrastructure;

Exclude all applicable taxes."[14]

The budget report and table have been reviewed and approved by the Deputy City Manager and Chief Financial Officer to ensure that appropriate estimates have been made. A funding strategy must also be developed to ensure sourcing of funding, such as "cost shared funding with other orders of government, other third party funding, development-related funding,"[15] and private stakeholder funding.

Nature of the Risk

There are a number of risks involved with the project that must be monitored and remedied to ensure the efficient and successful implementation of the Lawrence-Allen Revitalization Project. These have been identified as: community backlash to the project, height restrictions in the development area, passing zoning by-laws, phasing scheduling and cost estimates associated with the budget. Current residents of the Lawrence-Allen area may feel that they are being displaced from their homes due to the revitalization, however this aspect should be manageable. As discussed further in the paper, measures have been taken to ensure that community members have input into the revitalization process, thus allowing for a sense of control over the redevelopment of their neighbourhood. Certain design elements described by the Revitalization Plan represent increases in height or density over what is currently permitted in many areas. This is also of high-concern, as it could delay the building schedule of the project. Zoning By-Laws must be taken into consideration, as they could also affect the timely implementation of the project phases if not passed the first time. The reliability of the cost estimates in the budget table is of high importance, as significant cost increases could cause the project to go over-budget and stall the entire development process.

Keys to Success

Each of the phases of development, outlined above in the paper, will be required to pass Zoning By-laws as set out by the Planning Act and the City of Toronto Act before proceeding to the next stage of development. In particular, Sections 34, 37, 41 and 51 of the Planning Act and Section 114 of the City of Toronto Act. Zoning By-laws establish "permitted land uses, development rights, and performance standards for new buildings."[16]

5

The city will be required to undergo an application review process that will assess the proposed developments of each phase of the project. Public objectives and community benefits must also be clearly stated in the application for rezoning for it to pass. However, even after approval, holding provisions under Section 36 of the Planning Act, if used, may block development until specific facilities are in place or certain conditions met.[17] Also, each phase of the project will require plans of subdivision in compliance with Section 51 of the Planning Act, as well as, site plan approval on individual neighbourhood blocks within the core area, under Section 41 of the Planning Act and Section 114 of the City of Toronto Act. Lastly, it will need to satisfy the requirements of the Municipal Class Environmental assessment process, which falls under the Environmental Assessment Act. The Transportation and Infrastructure Master Plans will be in place to satisfy phases 1 and 2 of the above Environmental Assessment Act.

The Lawrence-Allen Revitalization Plan cannot be realized without cooperation and partnerships between the project's public and private stakeholders. The public stakeholders consist of other city divisions, and other public organizations, such as: Toronto Community Housing, TTC, Toronto District School Board, Toronto Catholic District School Board, Ministries of Transportation, Education, and Municipal Affairs and Housing.[18] The private stakeholders consist of major private landowners such as RioCan, Yorkdale, Baycrest Hospital, community residents, businesses, agencies and other special interest groups.

The reconfiguration of existing streets and blocks located in the main area of the revitalization project, Lawrence Heights, will require the cooperation of the three major public landowners, the City of Toronto, TCHC and the Toronto District School Board in developing a real estate strategy.[19] The strategy may necessitate further real estate transactions, apart from those already stated in proposal, by the three major landowners to successfully implement the revitalization plan. It will also have to be approved by the Ministry of Transportation and the Ministry of Environment. The support of senior levels of government will be required by the city and TCHC to full realize the housing objectives in the revitalization plan. There will have to be a rebalancing of the transportation system for the entire Lawrence-Allen area. This will require initiative and leadership from the TTC and a long term partnership with the private landowners Yorkdale, RioCan, and TCHC. It will also need support from the Ministry of Transportation.

The location of community facilities and the development of future centres will require partnership between the City of Toronto, Toronto Community Housing, TDSB, TCDSB, and the Ministry of Education. Community residents and agencies will also have to be actively involved in and participate in the design of the community facilities, as well as, parks, community projects, and other services. Public meetings have already been held to inform the neighbourhood residents about the project and to collect input and ideas, with the results from the meetings published to the project website or mailed to interested residents. In addition to various public meetings, tours of other already revitalized Toronto neighbourhoods have taken place, as well as, regularly scheduled newsletters and website updates. Current residents have also been hired by Toronto Community Housing to conduct surveys and focus groups in the many different spoken languages of the community to ensure that feedback is attained from all residents. A Community Advisory Group has been organized, with no political associations, to work with staff members and consultants from the City of Toronto, Toronto Community Housing, the Toronto District School Board and other stakeholders, "in areas such as transportation, parks, housing, community services, energy and sustainability."[20] Information displays for the public and the local residents have been arranged in many community buildings in the proposed area, including the New Heights Community Health Centre, the Toronto Community Housing building, the Lawrence Heights Community Recreation Centre and the Barbara Frum Library.

Considering the project area's proximity to the Downsview Airport, the flight path of arriving and departing airlines becomes an issue. Height restrictions for buildings in the area have been set out that include Lawrence Heights, as well as the entire Lawrence-Allen area. In order to avoid delays in building approval permits or re-planning, the height restriction guideline must be followed. If flight path height restrictions are changed in the future, "a comprehensive review of building heights should be completed before considering buildings taller than those anticipated by the Revitalization Plan."[21]

The Revitalization Project will require stringent monitoring and review over the course of its implementation. The planning application review process that is involved with each phase of the project will also allow for each phase to be thoroughly reviewed as the plan progresses. The successful implementation of the Lawrence-Allen Revitalization Plan will rely on phasing redevelopment to manage the many facets of revitalization, to ensure that development and growth does not outpace the municipal investment in the area that is needed to support intensification.

Assessment of Probability of Success

Similar communities that have undergone comparable revitalization projects, which have been turned into mixed communities, such as the Regent Park neighbourhood, St. Lawrence Market neighbourhood, and Harbourfront Bathurst Quay have been shown to be successful after revitalization was completed. In particular, the St. Lawrence Market neighbourhood, which was created in the late 1970's, serves as a model of design for mixed communities.[22] The neighbourhood has been critically acclaimed as a major success in urban planning and as a model of design and planning for new urban communities across North America. Harbourfront Bathurst Quay is another example of a mixed housing community which was developed in the 1990's with an assortment of housing types, shared school and community centre and parks, which has also shown to be successful after revitalization. Neighbourhoods such as Lawrence Heights, St. Lawrence Market, Regent Park and others were developed in the early years of housing development in Toronto and consequently, utilized a closed, high density method of design. Urban planners did not run streets through subsidized neighbourhoods based on these design standpoints. As a result, these types of neighbourhoods have become isolated, with "nowhere to work or shop, and at night these dead end streets turn into hotbeds of criminal activity."[23] It has become apparent that the old model of urban design is no longer applicable in today's environment; residents need to interact with other communities, have access to transit, public transportation and other resources in order to have a sustainable and successful community. The Lawrence-Allen Revitalization Project proposes to implement the necessary changes to accomplish this.

It appears that all of the necessary steps are in place for the successful redevelopment and revitalization of the Lawrence-Allen area. There has been initial co-operation between the many different stakeholders involved in the project, both private and public. There are programs and events being organized to involve the community in the project and receive community input. Moreover, extensive plans have been developed and are currently being further developed to ensure the timely and effective implementation of the revitalization project.

The Lawrence-Allen Revitalization Project will resurrect a once forgotten and deprived neighbourhood in the city's core. It is a neighbourhood that is comprised of the Lawrence Heights housing project, which is a distinct community in Toronto, with a diverse and vulnerable population. Reinvesting in the community and redeveloping it with current design standards will improve the delivery of community services, renew social housing for current residents as well as provide new housing for future demand. It will also build new public infrastructure in the area, parks and schools for its residents, and a functional transportation system. A comprehensive planning framework has also been developed to address all of the challenges facing the revitalization. The transformation of the neighbourhood into a successful, mixed community will help integrate it back into the broader city around it, and help manage to free itself from the social ills that have plagued it in its past.

Endnotes

[1] The City of Toronto, City Planning, *The Lawrence-Allen Revitalization Plan: Executive Summary* (Toronto: City Planning, 2010) 7.

[2] The City of Toronto, City Planning, *The Lawrence-Allen Revitalization Plan: Executive Summary* (Toronto: City Planning, 2010) 7.

[3] Donovan Vincent, "Massive Plan to Revamp Troubled Lawrence Heights," *The Toronto Star* [Toronto] 25 Feb. 2010.

[4] The City of Toronto, City Planning, *Lawrence-Allen Revitalization Project: Frequently Asked Questions* (Toronto: City Planning, 2008) 7.

[5] Donovan Vincent, "Massive Lawrence Heights Overhaul Planned," *The Toronto Star* [Toronto] 11 May 2007.

[6] The City of Toronto, City Planning, *Anticipated Growth Over 20 Years* (Toronto: City Planning, 2011) 1.

[7] The City of Toronto, City Planning, *Anticipated Growth Over 20 Years* (Toronto: City Planning, 2011) 1.

[8] The City of Toronto, City Planning, *Anticipated Growth Over 20 Years* (Toronto: City Planning, 2011) 1.

[9] The City of Toronto, City Planning, *Anticipated Growth Over 20 Years* (Toronto: City Planning, 2011) 1.

[10] The City of Toronto, City Planning, *Anticipated Growth Over 20 Years* (Toronto: City Planning, 2011) 1.

[11] The City of Toronto, City Planning, *Anticipated Growth Over 20 Years* (Toronto: City Planning, 2011) 1.

[12] The City of Toronto, City Planning, *Lawrence Allen Revitalization Plan Staff Report – June 3, 2010* (Toronto: City Planning, 2010) 5.

[13] The City of Toronto, City Planning, *Lawrence Allen Revitalization Plan Staff Report – June 3, 2010* (Toronto: City Planning, 2010) 22.

[14] The City of Toronto, City Planning, *Lawrence Allen Revitalization Plan Staff Report – June 3, 2010* (Toronto: City Planning, 2010) 3.

[15] The City of Toronto, City Planning, *Lawrence Allen Revitalization Plan Staff Report – June 3, 2010* (Toronto: City Planning, 2010) 23.

[16] The City of Toronto, City Planning, *Chapter 5: Making it Happen* (Toronto: City Planning, 2010) 1.

[17] The City of Toronto, City Planning, *Chapter 5: Making it Happen* (Toronto: City Planning, 2010) 1.

[18] The City of Toronto, City Planning, *Chapter 5: Making it Happen* (Toronto: City Planning, 2010) 1.

[19] The City of Toronto, City Planning, *Chapter 5: Making it Happen* (Toronto: City Planning, 2010) 4.

[20] The City of Toronto, City Planning, *Lawrence-Allen Revitalization Project: Frequently Asked Questions* (Toronto: City Planning, 2008) 7.

[21] The City of Toronto, City Planning, *Chapter 5: Making it Happen* (Toronto: City Planning, 2010) 4.

[22] David Gordon, *Directions for New Urban Neighbourhoods: Learning from St. Lawrence*, (Calgary: CIP/ACUPP Case Study Series, 1996): 2.

[23] Denise Balkissoon, "Plan to re-create Lawrence Heights Unveiled," *The Toronto Star* [Toronto] 25 Feb. 2010.